Water Habitats

Wetlands

JoAnn Early Macken

Reading consultant: Susan Nations, M. Ed.,
author, literacy coach, consultant

WR WEEKLY READER
EARLY LEARNING LIBRARY

Please visit our web site at: www.earlyliteracy.cc
For a free color catalog describing Weekly Reader® Early Learning Library's list of high-quality books, call 1-877-445-5824 (USA) or 1-800-387-3178 (Canada). Weekly Reader® Early Learning Library's fax: (414) 336-0164.

Library of Congress Cataloging-in-Publication Data

Macken, JoAnn Early, 1953-
    Wetlands / JoAnn Early Macken.
       p. cm. — (Water habitats)
    Includes bibliographical references and index.
    ISBN 0-8368-4887-X (lib. bdg.)
    ISBN 0-8368-4894-2 (softcover)
    1. Wetlands—Juvenile literature. I. Title.
QH87.3.M33   2005
578.768—dc22
                          2005047010

This edition first published in 2006 by
Weekly Reader® Early Learning Library
A Member of the WRC Media Family of Companies
330 West Olive Street, Suite 100
Milwaukee, WI 53212 USA

Copyright © 2006 by Weekly Reader® Early Learning Library

Art direction: Tammy West
Cover design and page layout: Kami Koenig
Picture research: Diane Laska-Swanke

Picture credits: Cover, pp. 7, 15, 21 © Tom and Pat Leeson; pp. 5, 9, 19 © Alan & Sandy Carey; p. 11 © Gustav Verderber/Visuals Unlimited; p. 13 © Bernard Castelein/naturepl.com; p. 17 © Dr. Fred Hossler/Visuals Unlimited

Printed in the United States of America

1 2 3 4 5 6 7 8 9 09 08 07 06 05

Note to Educators and Parents

Reading is such an exciting adventure for young children! They are beginning to integrate their oral language skills with written language. To encourage children along the path to early literacy, books must be colorful, engaging, and interesting; they should invite the young reader to explore both the print and the pictures.

Water Habitats is a new series designed to help children read about the plants and animals that thrive in and around water. Each book describes a different watery environment and some of its resident wildlife.

Each book is specially designed to support the young reader in the reading process. The familiar topics are appealing to young children and invite them to read — and reread — again and again. The full-color photographs and enhanced text further support the student during the reading process.

In addition to serving as wonderful picture books in schools, libraries, homes, and other places where children learn to love reading, these books are specifically intended to be read within an instructional guided reading group. This small group setting allows beginning readers to work with a fluent adult model as they make meaning from the text. After children develop fluency with the text and content, the book can be read independently. Children and adults alike will find these books supportive, engaging, and fun!

— Susan Nations, M.Ed., author, literacy coach,
and consultant in literacy development

A **marsh** is a wetland. Plants called cattails grow in a marsh. Their flowers look like cats' tails. Their long, thin leaves wave in the wind.

cattail

5

Muskrats build their homes from cattails, mud, and branches. They eat the cattail roots.

Birds eat cattails, too. Blackbirds build their nests among the **reeds**, or tall grasses.

cattail

A **bog** is a wetland. In a bog, moss grows on top of the water. Other plants grow on the moss.

moss

plant

In a bog, some plants eat insects. The plants catch insects in traps.

trap

13

A **swamp** is a wetland. Trees can grow in a swamp. Moss hangs down from the trees.

moss

Mosquitoes hatch in a swamp. Fish eat mosquitoes and their young, or **larvae**.

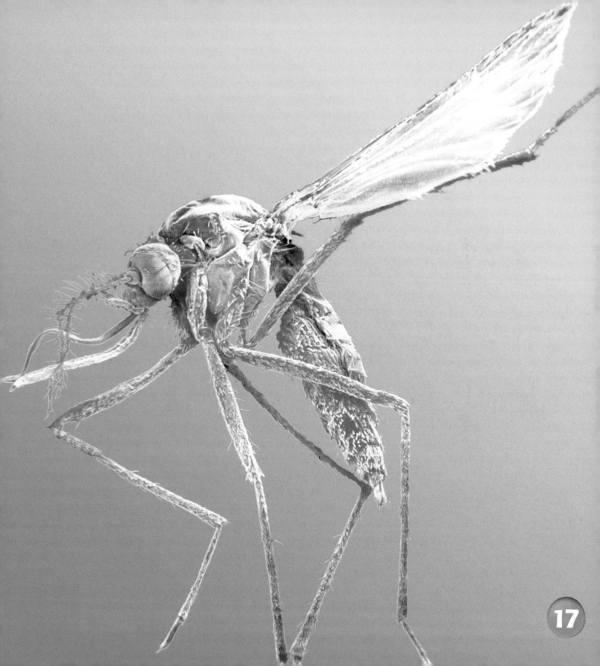

A heron wades on long, thin legs. It looks for fish or frogs to eat.

Alligators live in swamps.
They hunt under the water.
Their jaws snap up prey.
Watch out!

alligator

Glossary

bog — a wetland in which plants grow on a layer of moss

hatch — to break out of an egg

marsh — a wetland in which plants grow

mosquitoes — small buzzing insects that suck blood from animals

moss — small plants that grow in wet places

muskrats — rodents with shiny brown fur and long, thin tails

prey — an animal eaten by another animal

reeds — tall grasses that grow in wetlands

swamp — a wetland in which trees can grow

For More Information

Books

Life in a Wetland. Rookie Read-About Science (series). Allan Fowler (Children's Press)

Living near the Wetland. Rookie Read-About Geography (series). Donna Loughran (Children's Press)

Wetlands. Biomes of North America (series). Lynn M. Stone (Rourke)

Wetlands. We Can Read about Nature! (series). Catherine Nichols (Benchmark Books)

Web Site

Great Blue Heron

www.tpwd.state.tx.us/adv/kidspage/kidquiz/ wbirds/bluehero.htm

Pictures and information about great blue herons

Index

About the Author

JoAnn Early Macken is the author of two rhyming picture books, *Sing-Along Song* and *Cats on Judy*, and many other nonfiction books for beginning readers. Her poems have appeared in several children's magazines. A graduate of the M.F.A. in Writing for Children and Young Adults program at Vermont College, she lives in Wisconsin with her husband and their two sons. Visit her Web site at www.joannmacken.com.